Furious Cooking

Furious Cooking

POEMS BY MAUREEN SEATON

University of Iowa Press Iowa City

University of Iowa Press, Iowa City 52242

Copyright © 1996 by Maureen Seaton

Printed in the United States of America

Design by Richard Hendel

Printed on acid-free paper

Library of Congress Cataloging-in-Publication Data

Seaton, Maureen

Furious cooking: poems / by Maureen Seaton.

p.   cm.

ISBN 0-87745-541-4

I. Title.

PS3569.E218F8   1996

811'.54—dc20   95–46448

CIP

01   00   99   98   97   96   P   5   4   3   2

In memory of Gillis Duncan (d. 1590)

This idea of passing may be called time,

but it is an incorrect idea, for since one sees

it only as passing, one cannot understand

that it stays just where it is. —Dogen

Contents

The Red Hills   1

BLOOD

After Sinéad O'Connor Appears on *Saturday Night Live*, the Pope   4

Blonde Ambition   6

What She Thought   9

Cleaning St. Anne   11

Grace   13

Malleus Maleficarum   15

An Unofficial Interpretation of Pieter Aertsen's *A Butcher Stall
with the Holy Family Giving Alms on the Flight to Egypt*, c. 1550   16

Malleus Maleficarum 2   18

The Queen of Jersey   19

Malleus Maleficarum 3   21

Praxis   22

Malleus Maleficarum 4   24

Exquisite Corpse   25

Flash   27

A Brief History of Faith   28

WATER

Theories of Illusion   32

Eggshell Seas   35

Secrets of Water   37

Tagging   40

LA Dream #1   42

Will   44

LA Dream #2   45

A Single Subatomic Event   46

A Constant Dissolution of Molecules   48

LAVABO MANUS MEAS

Cannibal Women in the Avocado Jungle of Death   52

Called "Crass" by a Suitor during a Radically Conservative

    Moment in History, Helen Counsels Her Body   54

Slow Dance   56

Self-Portrait with Disasters   57

During the Eclipse I Remember You Sent Me *Playboy*   58

Swan Lake   60

The Sculpture Garden   62

Toy Car   64

The West Room   65

A Story of Stonewall   67

The Man Who Killed Himself to Avoid August   68

Femme-Butch Dialogue   70

A Chorus of Horizontals   72

Furious Cooking   73

Notes   75

Acknowledgments

These poems have appeared, some in different versions, in the following publications: *American Voice*, "Malleus Maleficarum"; *Boulevard*, "A Constant Dissolution of Molecules"; *Chicago Review*, "A Chorus of Horizontals"; *Columbia: A Magazine of Poetry & Prose*, "An Unofficial Interpretation of Pieter Aertsen's *A Butcher Stall with the Holy Family Giving Alms on the Flight to Egypt*, c. 1550" and "A Single Subatomic Event"; *Green Mountains Review*, "Toy Car"; *Harvard Review*, "LA Dream #1"; *Indiana Review*, "During the Eclipse I Remember You Sent Me *Playboy*," "Exquisite Corpse," "The Queen of Jersey," "The West Room," "Praxis," "Blonde Ambition," "*Cannibal Women in the Avocado Jungle of Death*," and "A Brief History of Faith"; *Iowa Review*, "Swan Lake," "Cleaning St. Anne," "Flash," and "Malleus Maleficarum 3"; *Massachusetts Review*, "The Man Who Killed Himself to Avoid August"; *Missouri Review*, "After Sinéad O'Connor Appears on *Saturday Night Live*, the Pope," "Eggshell Seas," and "Theories of Illusion"; *New England Review*, "Furious Cooking"; *Painted Bride Quarterly*, "Self-Portrait with Disasters"; *Paris Review*, "The Sculpture Garden" and "Slow Dance"; *Ploughshares*, "Secrets of Water"; *Prairie Schooner*, "LA Dream #2," "Tagging," and "What She Thought"; and *Ucross, the First Ten Years*, "The Red Hills." "Theories of Illusion" also appeared in *The Pushcart Prize XX: Best of the Small Presses*.

The author wishes to express her gratitude to the National Endowment for the Arts, the Illinois Arts Council, the Ragdale Foundation, and the Ucross Foundation for providing time, space, or funds for the conception and completion of this work.

Loving thanks are extended to Jennifer and Emily, Denise and Nick, Joan Marice Seaton (the Mother Witch), and all my collaborators at Woman Made Gallery and in *Postcards from the Inquisition*. And to H. P.

This is a work of fiction. The characters within the poems are not real, although references have been made to certain historical personages and events.

The power of the world is round:
bomb, uterus, cul-de-sac.
I sleep between breasts of earth
under the moon that rises. My life
is a circle in the high grass.

The devil creeps behind me.
There is something brilliant
about him. His hunger flares
for the smallest deer. He prowls
the red hills: See his light?

I name myself: Crazy Woman,
Wild Horse, Lightning Creek.
The devil trickles out of me
like blood on red earth,
leaves no trace.

These hills belong to him, they say,
but no one's here to testify.
The stones are silent, the creeks
murmur incoherently. I say:
In the darkness we are all holy.

Blood

After Sinéad O'Connor Appears on *Saturday Night Live*, the Pope

For Janet Bloch

The night we baptize the sidewalk outside Our Lady of Sorrows
across from Nelson's Funeral Home where the Neo-Futurists
spray-paint *Too Much Light Makes the Baby Go Blind,*

the only soul in sight is a woman with black eyes and bruises
staining her chin like grape juice. Perplexed, she leans
above a small figure stenciled on pavement and frowns.

Barb and Van and I are moving away from the church like clouds
up Clark toward Thybony Paints, which I always call "Thy bony,"
and we're stunned to hear her voice behind us say: "What's that?"

That is our simple rendering of a fifteenth-century criminal—
incantatrix, fascinatrix, malefica, sortilega, the one
who gathers herbs, charms, boxes of gooey sacred ointments.

When an old woman begins to doat and grow chargeable to a Parish,
she is generally turned into . . . a stick-rider, poisoner,
magus, hag, kasaph, evil eye, screech owl, night monster.

When a young woman goes *surfing* on a river in Essex, *to and fro,*
on a board standing firm bolt upright, turning and winding it
which way she pleases . . . , she is a strix, curandera, hocus-pocus.

When she heals a cold, braids her hair, unbraids it, breathes, dis-
respects a pope, has freckles, pockmarks, insect bites, cysts,
she's charged, raped, starved, robbed, beaten, drowned, burned.

"It's a woman," I say as our interloper gets close enough to touch.
The neighborhood looks so bloodless on a Wednesday night, its
citizens washed in TV, snug in bungalows and two-flats—

a ma-and-pa world, hard-working-hard-playing-fear-of-the-Lord
on a turquoise lake in the middle of turkey foot grass
and cornfields. Redeemed. Three witches embracing a fourth.

Blonde Ambition

The only miracle I ever wanted as a kid
was for my statue of Mary the Mother of God
to glow so I could feel enchanted.

I moved among grown-ups like a flame.
I was punctured by arrows of love,
I was boiled in consecrated oil, blameless

as risen Jesus, an anxious girl-child
of small radical expectations, sorry for sins
I'd never done. I stayed connected

to my he-lineage like a tiny fish
that lives on the benign whale shark
and follows him from ocean to ocean

in abiding complacency. Unlike *Colette*.
Or *Cher*. Now when I dream I'm flying
lonesome above other humans, striking

ballet poses and lifting off the floor
just enough so that they can't touch me,
I'm told I'm ambitious. Yet *Madonna*

scares me. I look at her peripherally
as if the radiance of her blonde ambition
is too bright or she might be contagious.

I'm told not to put her in a poem because
she will not endure the test of time,
she is no more deserving than Campbell's Soup

or the bee who gave his life when he
sank his pricker into my flesh. Meanwhile
I almost died on Friday at 5 on Half Day Road.

I used to tell my daughters not to worry,
no one dies until she's ready. For example:
My brakes gave out, I was closing in

on the windshield, the engine was moving
toward me like the will of God,
but I wasn't ready. I was totally alive

and dead at the same time. It was 1947.
I was about to be born, hovering
above two women strolling with sailors

in Elizabeth, New Jersey. One had the soul
of an angel. One the heart of a whore.
It was bright morning and the catbirds

were meowing in the old trees. The seaport
stank. I was waiting for someone more
immortal to stroll by, someone pregnant

with impossibilities. Is that a crime?
For example: You're allergic to bees.
The insect is heading toward your flesh

like a kamikaze pilot and kaboom
his essence is in your blood and driving
toward your vitals like a car with no brakes.

You: 1) Look around at your daughters
and memorize the exact radius of their eyes.
2) Examine your conscience and find it

spotless as your mother's kitchen floor.
3) Feel your death buzzing nuclear inside you,
fear lifting you up, cheeks hot with light.

What She Thought

Grandma, 85, is shot out of a circus cannon—and dies.

—Chicago tabloid, '94

I'm not exactly sure what to do with these bones sometimes they're so infused with a language impossible to translate but I know it means escape is inevitable. What happens to the bones of the old? Where does the phosphorus go? If our bones are replaced every few months where do the brittle bones of the old go? Red tells the story about his grandmother—how she fell against the living room couch and broke her neck. In front of the whole family. On Thanksgiving. My bones are dispersing as I speak.

Sweet irreverence, sweet obstacle.

I remember how my blood smelled after I gave birth—good dirt and the secrets of water— and no one could come near me but the child who arrived in its flow, the daughter launched into fluorescence beside the husband who survived on Rusty Nails.

Let us pray: Here where the water bubbles in the large-capacity pot like a rage beginning.

How connected woman to her blood, how we seek or refuse the tie. Once I lost my blood for five years. There were no swings, and the feathers that grew on my lips and arms were slicked with sweet-smelling oil. I tasted of bread.

I said: Kiss this.

I was in the car and we were driving between New Jersey and New York. I was caught between a mother and a father. I was crossing my ankles like a ballerina. There were so many things to think about. That morning I had awakened and thought of all the people in the entire world, how on the seventh day God created them.

Today the energy is a flow to the top of my head the sweet adrenaline and all the rose in my face like the opposite of fossils or maybe fossils bloom in the cheek exactly like a flush of wanting I am so gone let me repeat the energy is at the top of my head the crown the foolscap the hair parted down the middle and aside from the tips of fingers and the sport of staying awake even when the world around me dozes off.

Cleaning St. Anne

St. Anne holds Mary on her ample impastoed lap,
they're both grown but Anne's got knees
the size of ham bones and Mary's light as a conscience.

They say Leonardo painted with his fingertips,
dragged the paint across the surface, blending one tone
into another, precious pigment into sealer.

Everyone's barefoot and plump, reclining
on high rocks somewhere higher than Montana.
Jesus is squeezing a lamb. Mary reaches out placidly.

I love St. Anne this way, butch and nurturing.
How will her restorers decide what's actual varnish
and what's original pigment? That's the question.

I moved into St. Anne's parish in 1958.
I hadn't been tweaked or rulered yet, no one'd
threatened me with sadism or molested my little brother.

Now her head is cracking badly, she needs
analysis and restoration, the paint above her eyes thin
as mother's milk, her daughter's robes greasy as makeup.

I say: It's women who keep the church alive.
There we are, week after week, filling the pews,
handing men the reins. What do we expect?

Still, there is little left between modesty and acrimony,
little that the cruciform does not polarize
like a magnet in iron filings—you here, you here.

Transcendence comes late, well after seven, that
age of reason when you're finally able, after games
of catechism, to figure out equations for salvation.

Honey, you need a good cleaning. Your face
is covered with a dark green veil and your eyes
have lost their watery sheen. Mona Lisa's next, and look

at *Ginevra de'Benci*, cross-eyed as the day she was born,
now pearly as a baby's behind. The tints of her face
appear not to be colors at all—but living breathing flesh.

Grace

I
You can find the child striking matches in the sanctuary. She has waited her
whole life for the danger. She ages in the cool myrrh amid ghostly whisperings.
She thinks: *The living hold more dread.* She doesn't really think this but she
doesn't budge. Mary swims in blood light, the child's sins are shadowy. Still, she
creates her own confession. *Our Father, Hail Mary.* Her contrition buds perfect
as the Infant's toes.

II
Things they slap her for: *Our Father who art in heaven Howard be thy name, two
men walking a breast,* hair in her eyes, talking to boys, gum, failure to curtsy,
marbles in her mouth, passing notes, talking to Jane Ellen, smirking, ducking,
telling her mother that Sister Patricia pulled Jane Ellen's ponytail really hard for
missing a math problem, reading the word *bowels* instead of *bowls* by mistake
then laughing hysterically.

III
How Jane Ellen's head looked like a doll's head and almost popped off.
How Patricia disciplined the boys in the boiler room with their pants down.
How there was nothing I didn't already know and all the words in all the books
and all the numbers and all the equations rescued me from Christ's body
and from the winged angels and the bloody saints and Almighty God Himself.
How

IV

one day the lights went out on the East Coast, up and down the rivers and
streets, you could feel the hush as it all shut down, every last elevator, every
known form of transportation. You could ride the dark, you could calculate
distances between bodies but not well and, this is important, you could not
see your hand at all.

V

Thus, with an abandon impossible in lesser states of grace, the child went forth
and sinned. *In nomine Patris, et Filii, et Spiritus Sancti. Amen.*

VI

This is the trouble with modern-day grace, it's household and promiscuous,
nothing tucked away and stealthy about it, nothing canonical or ex cathedra.
Holy Mother of a Sucking Louse. You can say this millions of times, try it, and
still the lights will flicker one day, flare the next, and you'll be somewhere in the
middle with your small faiths, the way even heaven can seem burlesque, so epic
and clean.

Malleus Maleficarum

My hands have been worried for days,
sticky old-fashioned flypaper, palms

pulsing like corks in wine bottles
buried in cobwebby corners about to burst.

Like gunshots. Like a youngster's guts spilled
on the sidewalk of the Lincoln Avenue bridge.

I caused nothing, simpletons, yet you rush
to apply thumbscrews to make confession

inevitable. I can prevent none of this,
not the boy's death I feel in my hands as if

he were my own son, nor the lies you stuff
in my mouth from your wormy handbook:

crimes, sorcery, names, spells. We drove,
my friend and I, to the bridge across the river.

The blood was there, rusting in the sun,
and the citizens were walking back and forth

as if this weren't a window to the universe.
We threw flowers in the current, that's all.

No magic. A gorgeous bird dove for a fish
then flew south. A boat sped by with three

drunk men. My friend knelt down and touched
the blood. I watched the river. We drove away.

An Unofficial Interpretation of Pieter Aertsen's *A Butcher Stall with the Holy Family Giving Alms on the Flight to Egypt*, c. 1550

For Jennie

I can almost understand his disparate incorporation
of the alleged Mother of God into the side of beef, eye of lamb,
fly-inhabited slab of a painting in every shade of blood.

But mankind's progression from worldly pleasure
to spiritual nourishment? Pork hock, calf leg, chicken neck,
Christ? The Madonna doling out coins in the center window

framed by mutton and sausage links of the Netherlandish School
may be an enviable juxtaposition for any symbolist.
But raw meat in high summer "slash" heavenly sustenance?

Imagine Piet in love with alizarin crimson, despondent
over the gored saints of his failing iconography,
the suppositions of Inquisitional pomp and jurisprudence.

Imagine the butcher shop transcendent as a plea, his mind
like any bard's in a warp of fascistic intolerance.
Imagine you're a Dutchman confined to virgins and churches

and gray congregations climbing soft hills to feast
on broken bodies, the stored clarets of sanctuary cupboards
washing down sticky flesh and arbitrary dogma.

Your wife has died of heresy, no saint, believe me, only
touched by a long finger extended from the See
of Rome all the way to Amsterdam. How odd. How sick.

Her only faults beauty and song and still you watched her
burn like a flank of deer for the triune God
she murmured in your ear at night. Imagine the plight

of holy men, Pieter in the butcher's stall with all those
puddles on the floor like spilled wine, the stench deepening
in the day's heat, all those dead eyes slanting toward peace.

Malleus Maleficarum 2

I'm supposed to be the witch in this scenario,
all points and hard angles, big evil plans.

Sure I'm near death and like to cook, so what?
I was kind to a priest once, red-haired

kid himself, freaked him out, that's all.
Neither of us believed in God after that,

not your God at least, that greedy awkward
preacher around the subject of sex broken

like the legs of a whore, the toes of a virgin.
All women can heal, you dolts, our spit

can make a blind man weep. We invented
holy mud, the cave, the pool, the temple

where you took your bodies for centuries
and lay them down beside us. We raised you

from death and birth, you dreary bootlickers,
kept our hair in braids at your request,

controlled seas, crops, angels of doomsday.
Oh, dull prickers, you can pluck every strand,

beat our children as they watch us burn,
six generations of them—imagine their souls

transplanted into stars shining down on us—
and still, sirs, you will die without pockets.

The Queen of Jersey

I

Last night Diana tottered over the brink and, leaning as if on oil, said:
I still sin though full I be.

II

Glisten river, the same light that flares over Newark flares tonight as she vomits
through barbed wire into your chilled dark. She's gorgeous in her bones and
blue as china. Drear river—edge of confession, hard candy mouth, fructifying
glimpse of What Waits.

III

There is a tapioca wind pocked wind loose there is a nauseous wind who would
sit so close I can feel its breath on my neck like a monsoon I am so fed up with
wind sticky like a popsicle wind never mind crumpled paper zooming along in
sickly wind the complications of all that air coming from the west beating down
the shopping malls I hate you wind you blow so sacred and obstinate you leave
me pressed against walls with my face blown away my throat puking wind there
is nothing solid about you I can't stand you holy wind sacred lip of God oh God
you come and come you are no one I can hang on to.

IV

She said: Kiss this.

V

In the hospital, the glory of Diana playing Queen of Hearts, Queen of Diamonds—
those red moms—playing with the nurses' eyes because she is yes she is in so
much pain she needs watching. I can't bear all this hair on my body like the fur
animal activists spray and slash. Is it better to die with fat on your bones, greasy
and plump as mountains with oil sliding down?

VI

Everything you ever hoped for could come crashing in like God's foot while he lies in heaven with his big cigar and his TV blasting static.

VII

She said: Here is the soul of What To Do. Here is the turnpike ticking and clicking. The eagle claws about to drop you, light-headed, onto the floor of Jersey. There is nothing better than the flame above the oil refineries, the wail and perfume of home-sweet-home.

VIII

The green swamp? The gray curls of smoke above the Budweiser factory? The Budweiser eagle? Jelly donuts in the pocket? Sugar on the chin?

IX

She said: There is nothing I would ever do to harm you.

Malleus Maleficarum 3

Let me tell you what it's like with a goat,
gentlemen, his officious member wagging

upward, the spleen in his eyes requiring
coma on my part, the thrill flagged before

his first bleat. He carried me
up the stairs to my bed which lay squarely

on the floor like any sixties witch's pad,
and took me there in full earshot of every

saint I conjured up to ice him instantly
before my babies climbed their crib bars

and toddled down the hall. Who
knew cavorting against one's will

could be such an obstacle to grace—that
stench-filled dance on his part, turbid gulps

of time travel on mine. I see it now:
the mom, the kids, sucking snow in a strange

landscape. The snow is blue in paper cups.
I think it's Coney Island before the flood,

there's a horse diving into waves, salt
for floating, cotton candy, franks. "Hot

enough for you?" the tanning people say,
my body nestled in wool, in fire.

Praxis

For Judith Arcana

Even in imperceptible petticoats I had a vision I was striking the earth
and all around were the deliberate actions of birds, there were two

big ones taunting from a low branch, I thought that—taunting—
they could be crows or grackles though crows are more imposing

than the common grackle (both deliberate as judges, however)—
where was the iridescence that would distinguish grackle from crow?—

and they just sat there taunting from the lowest branch, the white
oak's wizened wrist, it was fall and nothing I'd tried had worked.

First I'd tried tuck-pointing. The strategy there was reverse perspective.
I thought: Let me learn the spaces between the bricks, then

I'll be informed regarding the nature of architecture, its Zen and yin,
you can build an entire building, I thought, and never know its name.

But still I was the same petticoated yearling, there was nothing perceivably
different in my worldly perceptions, you could count my knowledge

in the lightning time it took grackles to switch their flight pattern.
I observed a single leaf on the old oak, the way it hung there

in its terrible gravity unsure if the ground were home or hell, and what,
I thought, is meant by the infinitive *to ransom* when followed by the word

death anyway? I'd taken a trip to Indiana and observed an artist
duplicating the Sistine Chapel in his studio, the ache

of Adam, the fingertip of God. I took up the brush myself
and duplicated *Sleeping Venus*. I thought her body would make me wise.

I watched the common grackles rise from the oaks with infamous
synchronicity, this way, that, uncommon as dancers or Olympians,

I watched the two taunting birds busy themselves with preening and cant.
Crows, I thought, it was good to finally be sure. But oils and tuck-pointing

weren't the only means to an end and over the years I'd layered one
action on another and my petticoats were so bulky now no one could trust me

to walk a sober line. Instead, I zagged and zigged, you may not believe this,
but sometimes I'd lie down in the middle of a pile of leaves and sleep! Finally

I drew the Five of Swords and my friend *la curandera* said: "You are using
the wrong tools or you are using the tools in the wrong way or the tools

you have been using are for the birds, my friend." And she vanished
like a yellow leaf in the earth's lap. The birds were grackles.

You can still see them preening, shouting. The End. Grackles
pretending to be crows.

Malleus Maleficarum 4

Now you lean across the table, fingers
gold and sticky with apricot preserves,

dishing up the third degree. *At the Witches'*
Tower in Hesse, victims were hung

fifteen feet above ground in niches, slowly
baked to death over a low fire. I'm

infected with a nasty tongue, you say,
heresy the devil himself must have loosed,

the nerve to intuit insanity. Wolfenbuttel,
Germany, 1590: *There were so many stakes . . .*

the place resembled a small forest. Como:
one thousand dead. Strasbourg: five thousand.

Nine million women over three hundred years.
What's one more, father? I'll tell you

about magic. It's the slow ticking
of a woman's heels on deserted city streets,

hair haloed in cold lamplight, eyelids
heavy with Chicago river smog. The knife

she carries against her hip is subtle as sin
and nothing bad will happen to her tonight

for she knows how to snap the blade, like this,
and carry you with her into hell.

Exquisite Corpse

The spicy watch wandered the slimy painting
in sexy stockings women wear in movies that
come up and over the knee and never fall down, never.
Here is the point of the slimy painting and here
is the time on the spicy watch: birth, death, surgery.
The doctor chases her around the room and her stockings
never fall down, never. As spicy as she is she dies
young as a movie star and all her slimy paintings
wander among us like veins, up and over the knee,
around the ears, down the neck and disappear
into our blouses between our breasts and down
even further until we are egg and smear and satisfied.
I fear the colors of blood and often dream of them,
a white woman with crimson in her gene pool—
gore, clot, plasma, vampire, varicose, hemal, leech.
Some of my blood burned women at the stake
for the nasty crime of healing, some of my blood said *kike*
at the dinner table while slicing roast beef. *Nigger*
wop dago chink. Some of my blood raped their wives
in the first week of marriage. Then they raped their slaves,
then their slaves' children, then their wives' children.
Then they fenced in the earth and everything
belonged to my blood—carcass, corpus, languid, sallow,
zombi, mummy, ghost. Frida's friends and family
photographed the artist after she died—strange to my blood
as visiting graves on the Day of the Dead. We'd
rather build a shopping mall over our grandfathers' heads,
pay them no mind—try to find us in suburbia, Death.

Here is the point of the slimy painting and here is the time
on the spicy watch: Blood, eternal as an ancestor.
The exquisite corpse shall drink the new wine,
the wounded woman disturb the guillotine with her hair.
The flame-coloured breast surpasses by one step, one
finger, one mouthful . . .

Flash

This female life is such a secret vernacular, I'm so slinky and sneaky, prowling the heat of Broadway with my invisible spear. The heat begins inside, radiates down my legs and up into my eyes till I'm crazy with restricted information, discreet as a hand circling a vulva. Soon no ova will descend the little tubes shaped like music, leap from the ganglia near the cashew-shaped ovaries, and break into the womb's dark clearing. The first time I masturbated, I thought I'd cheated on my then-husband, Ricardo. Someone had finally provided enough foreplay for me to reach the cliff and jump! That night I felt the fetus like a swimming in the dark of uterus and soul, nibbling at my insides, no, a knock at a tiny door, a tiny knock, lots of them, alien hands pulling taffy back and forth, scritch-scratching on a chalk board. *No one can feel this but me* I thought but it felt like a scream and no one could hear that either. Who would believe the end wraps itself around the beginning, that I am ruled by hormones, this heat an ovum, the way the egg slips, incognito, into the cool obsolete, tinier now than a teaspoon's shadow.

A Brief History of Faith

(She faints at the altar rail)

Someday I will be a martyr for my faith, I know it, because I get afraid at night and the statues near my bed glow, I swear—the Little Flower, Mary, Jesus. I kneel for hours with my rosary, I know all the mysteries, the glorious ones are my favorite but I save them for special days. I know the stations of the cross by heart, I can say the entire Mass in Latin. When they change the rules I will be the first lady priest, then I will be a monsignor, then a bishop, then a cardinal. Wanna know what happens to me if I don't faint? Okay. The priest puts the host on my tongue and I get ready, because once Jesus slides down my throat it gets dark and I can't see very well. I mean, my eyes are closed and I can't see where I'm going but I go somewhere far away through a tunnel real fast. Sister says sit down with the other children, communion's over. I feel embarrassed and my freckles blend. If I faint they carry me out and lay me on the grass. I feel light as a robin, I feel safe.

(She fasts from midnight)

Here is the ghetto of St. Anne's Parish with my house on the extreme east side. It's a ghetto with a theme—follow it west and you'll find the children in my eighth grade class on collegiate streets like Dartmouth, Harvard, Princeton—Kathy on Yale, Liz on Oxford. We all go to St. Anne's School and we all attend St. Anne's Church with our families on Sunday, fasting from midnight so we can swallow the Body of Christ and not defile Him with pulverized food in our stomachs. Once I forgot and licked a lollypop and was forbidden to take communion that day—punishment equivalent to hanging out in the stocks of Old England. Whenever someone asks you where you live you say: *Saint So-and-So's.* Everything is Parish. The Priest is God. My Father is God's Right-

Hand Man. I grow up ladylike, obedient, practice the piano, don't talk back. It's 1968 (it's 1990). Marriage is my only career option.

(She follows her vocation)

You can see the way I look in home movies, strained and jaundiced, rib cage showing through my sundress, hair in place. When Rick gets home we drink gin and tonics in summer, whiskey sours in winter. I wake up Sunday mornings with hangovers, the kind where the whole world is in your ears and your body feels like the flu only guilty. Jennie has nightmares from age two to six, the normal age according to Freud. I'm sitting on the front porch drinking, Rick is making tall drinks with lots of lime, and it eases itself in, that gin. Go to sleep, I say to Jennie because I am so tired and it's the end of the day and my well is dry. I say, oh God, go to sleep, and I melt into the chair until I am the chair and her nightmares fly over my head like a prayer and never touch me.

(She dies)

I went down to put my whites in the laundry and there were three men on the elevator, all wet with raindrops. So I said, "It's raining?" And they were so happy to say yes. Isn't it wonderful how one minute you think it will be sunny forever, infinity, and the next there is rain on your shoulders and head and people to notice and that's what comforts humanity, small talk and rain? Last night I saw a woman of advanced age with a tee shirt that said *Finity*, and I wondered what that meant to her. That her life was almost over and she would soon die and that was okay with her? I love the idea that nothing separates us from each other. I put my hands on a dying woman once and felt her soul burning around her and touching me back in a way the woman's body was unable to. Her soul was huge. I could feel it as I came down the hall, long before they told me she was starving, and we spoke of the weather, the surprise of it all, the way it changed.

(She walks down Broadway)

There is a continual motion like a movement of Bach there is music to die by music to kill over no one looks at you when you get old there is that whole set of thrills you lose as you walk down the street Oh one or two vendors an occasional homeless but you can't quite believe them yesterday there was a man reading Hardy on 116 holding out a paper cup I just came down from Grant's tomb Ulysses and Julia in their flashy coffins all that hoopla about the old boy's righteousness you can still tell a human being by the eyes the eyes let's say there is good in this world and if you want it go down the steps past the old gentleman who lives beneath the columns by the tomb keep going and the river will begin to stink you can't miss it the cool will hit you in the face the movement like a fugue the way your hands answer each other listen there are oboes if you're quiet remember how you thought you'd never find love

Water

Theories of Illusion

The panda has a sixth digit we call
a thumb but really it's a greatly enlarged
radial sesamoid, a simple component of the wrist.

Also, although the panda is a charter member
of the order Carnivora, she eats absolutely nothing
but bamboo from the mountains of western China.

As for the orchid, we may think *brava!*
What an amazingly well thought out system
for attracting insects. But it's no more

than a zany arrangement of already existing
flower parts, a jury-rig of pistil and stamen—
much like my ex-boyfriend, Will, in his many disguises

in and around America, the chilling fact
that he's absolutely Will but can pass for someone
or something else. For example, while bodybuilding,

Will can be heard grunting in his makeshift gym
until his back looks apeish, his calves
like a goat's leaping on high places. He can easily

be mistaken for Chinese, Cherokee, Greek, that
might be him right now looking Latino near Montrose.
He used to say he'd find me one day and I'd never

recognize him until he had me pinned in bed.
He said, "The strong survive," like the placentals
who roamed across the Isthmus of Panama

and all but extinguished the marsupials—
and then he'd squeeze me for luck and punctuation.
Once he was sitting in a saloon after escaping

from a hospital on the Hudson, and a cop asked him,
point-blank, if he'd seen himself. Like a slippery hero,
a quantum leap of light, energy radiating

at different levels of illusion, an insane
physics: Mad Max meets Inspector Clouseau. Once
the dinosaur was ineluctable as dawn

and all the big ones lumbered and the winged ones
tried to fly, and for a hundred million years they reigned,
fit and fervent as the myth of creation.

Now their descendant sparrow zooms above Swan Lake
like a fairy spirit of the coelurosaurus,
and the orchid continues expensive as silk.

Now the panda faces starvation, and some believe
Will has taken his life in Montana after a day of fishing.
My favorite illusion is the one about the relativity

of time. How the humpback with her big slow heart,
her contrapuntal biorhythm, weaves a song in the deep—
half-hour concert to us, to her a minute waltz.

Eggshell Seas

Gloria thinks it's particularly smart
the way Californians refuse to clutter
their winding roads with safety features
that encourage tourists to clog America—
Atlantic couples who swear they prefer slate seas,
big Midwestern corn-fed types
with their eyes on the seventy slick miles
of mountain and cliff where anyone could fall,
just nudge that Cavalier to the right
and you're seaweed, the light around you
thick and blonde as perfect hair. Gloria
thinks nothing could be more religious
than doing sixty past Seal Rock and Bird
where the fog breathes on your windshield
like an angel and everyone else is creeping
down Route 1 as if this life were connected
to some kind of justice. Romantically,
she slips around Cypress Point,
flirts with sea lions and harbor police. It's
her first time out of cities but she's
no slouch at veering to avoid harassing bulks
or the occasional cigar smoke
that threatens to oust her from the pavement,
that well-worn line from home to job,
cinema, supermarket, therapy, Workout World,
all those sundries city folk fit around them
like crib bars so they won't fall off the earth.
She thinks this sea is beautiful,

lapis lazuli and green vein combined, not to mention
the pearl she swallows like an oyster
that fastens to her insides, ready for descent.

Secrets of Water

For Jeanette Mason
(Polymorphous perverse and highly intelligent, dolphins of both genders prefer
sex play with the human female.)

I

Water begins from a wound in the hillside, a tear in the clouds.
There's a tin cup no one cares has years of germs on its icy rim.

The water is sweeter than anything you will ever hold in your mouth.
And the spring doesn't start then stop. It's tireless and beneficent

yet nothing you do can make it love you in a different way—warmer
or more solid. The ocean held me under and I began to look around.

Everything looked like a world, not just a place to play. It was real,
separate from the air-world or the bonfire-world. I struggled, of course,

but noticed amazing things. How it must seem to a fish to go backward
into the mouth of a great white shark, painlessly, as if the shark

were swallowing it whole. The sea was thick with light and people's legs
near shore were huge as pipelines and skinny as worms. The sun

was a memory, or the sun was a needle pushing gently through foam.
When you're drowning you cannot close your eyes for anything. You want

to look forever. There are your legs, frantic beneath you, and ten toes
licking the dark like little tongues. Your neck stretches out, chest

expands, everything about your body begins to bud and sing, hair
billowing gorgeously. Your debts don't matter, your hot flashes. Sand's

everywhere—crotch, cleavage, corners of your eyes. Such beauty,
and your fear so dazzling, benign. When they finally pull you out,

your lungs vomit sea into their beloved faces and they lean toward you,
like suns, asking are you okay. Their language breaks your heart.

II

I keep thinking of my dead ex, Will, his circular life of Russian roulette,
that expulsion of singed air like breath from a slaughtered seacalf—

what comes to us in our meat and in our sewers—something pale
and ferocious rolling over and over in the shadows: chiaroscuro.

Black cars pass me on the Sprain Brook—a Toyota with four-wheel drive—
and I remember how Will took me to Fahnestock Park and we made love

in the back of his pickup. We were stretched across the Appalachian Trail
like islands and he was right—he'd never make it to forty. All this

fog around our bodies like the dreams of a thousand trout. We were wading
in the stream. We were hooking ourselves and throwing ourselves back in.

III

The dolphin circles amiably. He has discovered my scent, my energy,
I can hear his sonar clicking like a child's toy, muffled and patient.

They say he can locate a metal plate in the brain, a pacemaker in the heart,
he's so bitingly intelligent the shark sighs and turns away. Still,

his penis brushing the back of my knee terrifies. I know he wants only
to play, to nudge and pull, sharing me with his curious mate, three

divine fishes easing through blue wake, skin like opals and quicksilver.
Will was slick with secrets. They hid beneath his skin, sloshing and feverish

as if his body were a cauldron or a dying star. He was a flawless lover,
coolest draft, generous as a flood, gifted with a global sensuality

that washed away continents and lives. He held me and his ribs were enormous,
impossible to hug all the way around, slippery as a cliff's wet face.

I thought this would feel religious—two species communing in a womb of salt.
Now six hundred pounds of mammal clock me as I backstroke to safety—

oxygen, earth, and fire pursued by lust and innocence. The ocean is opaque.
Bubbles float to the top and break like oracles from a lost treasure.

Tagging

There's something we've named a game show with all kinds of dings and glitches
going on in the next room, and outside the Queen of Angels points her steeple

at something we call heaven. We say Chicago's more polite than New York.
Driving around, you sometimes find a person who will give you a break.

He or she will signal for you to pull out in front, and if you're from New York,
you will wave and wave until he or she is lost in your rearview mirror. We say

we're safer here. Lately I've been reading something called the *new* physics,
the kind where nothing's sure and that's just fine with us: dissipative structures,

inconclusive theories, discontinuous motion—one big *huh?* at time and space,
one small question leading to others we ask and ask until we're giddy, all those

unexpected foldings into a seamless universe. We say brazen electrons leaping
into invisible orbits. We say blood invisible as Jesus. I was stardust

when the first atom exploded on Chicago's South Side. Now
our children discover ways to kill each other without metal—they scoot

through detectors like excited hydrogen, armed with plastic guns called gats.
They scatter down Clark and land beneath a sheet outside our doors.

Their wars are small, American. They name themselves *the people* and *the folks*,
tag the land because nothing's left that's free. Nothing in the universe

exists separately, we say—us, our kids, fear, blood, grief. First,
a man and a woman spin a wheel and then they try to guess a phrase, and if

they're lucky they win a car or money. We call this *The Wheel of Fortune.*
I'm holding my breath as an architect from Los Angeles uncovers a rush

of vowels. I love the vowel *a.* It's round or flat and beautiful and free.
In New York we say cat, hat, tobacco. In Chicago we say cat, hat, tobacco.

We say we are dissolving into sky, our breath is piquant with rumors,
our whole body frantic for the leap and the sweet light that follows.

LA Dream #1

My son is killed by a train and becomes
a marble in my back tooth although
no one will believe this, I am so well-
dressed, so civilized and harmless.

Next I am chopping dead chickens
in the scenery room at Warner Brothers.
My boy's face appears on a block of frozen parts.
The atmosphere is smothered fear.

Take me again through the city clean
and organized as Beverly Hills after dark.
This is where the rich live, the poor. The child,
my son beneath the train, a bloody spot,

has leapt to the river and we go there,
hoping to find him beneath the ice
frozen in expectation. In this other life
I have no son. Yet here we are

chasing all over the dream for a skinny kid.
He's so sweet he could grow up
just like Henry Fonda or Gregory Peck,
remember them? This dream city

is filled with musicians. They meet me
at the elevator like a backdraft of fire.
I am music myself when they embrace me,
and I know this is the place to be.

Yesterday in 1994 Chicago
I heard harmonica on the subway platform.
The dollar I slipped inside his guitar case
might buy him six rolls at the bakery

or he might save and save for the night
he can lose himself in one smoky moment.
My dollar, his music. Which is richer?
If he were in the dream in this city,

connected like Los Angeles, in this room
for make-believe like Warner Brothers,
he would be valued and play his harmonica
for all the children. He would eat like a producer.

When he opened his mouth to sing, a boy
would walk along the railroad tracks humming,
and when the train came by, hungry as God,
he'd brush it away like a feather, a song.

Will

He's uncertain if someone said *Hey* last night while he ran down the escalator that appeared miraculously on 96th Street or now as he pushes the electronic door with his arms full of last-minute things. The world is gorgeous from great heights—the geometry, punctuation, infinite lines of blurred incandescence. He's flying now, dream or real, straight for that shock of tulips on 99th Street, missing the rheumy Siamese who wonders *Me*? The clot of schoolchildren waiting for the Broadway bus. The woman who just held up Love's Pharmacy. He's that concerned with color, composition, depth.

LA Dream #2

I was on the left side of the dream which was three-dimensional as all dreams I was watching myself on the left side of the dream I could not see my head but it was me as it is in all dreams and so my eyes were not visible yet the body was mine stretched out on a kind of bed or a bench this is always confusing this detail but it seemed wooden I don't know the period of the dream but I think it was a bench or a pew and I was naked. In the middle of the dream that is in the middle of the screen of the dream I could see a child who Freud (Jung?) said is also me and she could have been her bangs familiar her pixie face she was so little perhaps three or four the phallic stage though truly without a phallus in fact there was no phallus visible in the dream which did not detract the least from the fear. I'm sorry I told you the faint of heart must exit here or the very pure of spirit you may want to close your eyes because what happens next is so devastating and I myself the creator of the dream could not believe it upon waking but also could not deny the sequence of events how the little girl who was me climbed on top of the woman who was me and there was a flash of sex. How terrifying to me the woman both in the dream and in the moment I woke beside the electric fireplace grounded on a street that dead-ends on a river in Chicago. I put the child down on the floor at once and that's crucial but listen I don't know if this is important but listen I can understand now why some people hurt children I can understand the child wanting love so much she will open everything I understand how a woman confuses desire and forgets this is a child I understand now I don't want to but I do the universe gave me the body and the child and the camera and told me go ahead and shoot.

A Single Subatomic Event

In memoriam: Barry Siebelt (1945–1994)
There is no way you can use the word reality *without quotation marks around it.*
—*Joseph Campbell*

Imagine two concentric cylinders with a liquid like glycerine
in the snug space between them. Drop a small circle

of ink into the glycerine and rotate the apparatus slowly.
See how the ink is drawn into a thin black line,

how it fades, invisible as the energy it takes to ponder reality.
I like reality, it tastes of bread. The path exists only when we observe it.

We expect so much from the dead; or we expect so much less
than the dead can give. One theory of reality implies

a folding of atoms, humans, tea cozies inside a seamless universe,
objects we can't see, hear, etc., right at our collective noses.

Who can measure the distance between us and the dead? How many arias
in an oratorio? *What is crucial, according to the theory of relativity,*

is that a sharp distinction between space and time cannot be maintained.
When told to "get real," I instinctively turned my head to right and left

so my eyes and ears could catch something invisible, inaudible:
a hum so close I could hug it, and beneath the hum

that cache where the universe stores its music. Einstein
could be heard laughing over the flaws of relativity. Something

does travel faster than the speed of light, can you believe it?
Two particles, once in contact, separated even to the ends of the universe,

change instantaneously when a change occurs in one. There are more
arias than you can count, right, Barry? Let me tell you,

when I rotated those cylinders in reverse I held my breath. Not
that I expected disappointment, but when that fine black line reappeared,

teasing me like the lonesome tail of a memory, I understood
about the speed of light, how you defied it and spun away,

and all the cities between us stood tall at your departure, every cow
and turtle. Now we see you. Now we will see you again.

A Constant Dissolution of Molecules

Some tissue, such as bone, is especially dynamic. Each body structure has its own rate
of reformation: the lining of the stomach renews itself in a week; the skin is entirely
replaced in a month; the liver is regenerated in six weeks. . . . after five years one can
presume that the entire body is renewed, even to the very last atom.
—*Larry Dossey,* Space, Time, and Medicine

My lovers blur. They say, for instance: "You are too good to be true."
They stand beneath the bells of Queen of Angels at noon
and pretend the noise hurts their ears. They make faces like Chaplin,
like Desi Arnaz. Their right thighs have been used for skin grafts
although *she* was burned in a campfire, *she* almost lost an arm.
There were any number of accidents involving my lovers
on something strong like Bacardi, something weak like Colt 45.
One fell between the cars of the 2 train, one went through a windshield.
No, two went through a windshield. One landed on the hood of a truck,
one on the pavement in the middle of the Tappan Zee Bridge.
Here are the scars, here are the keloids, here are the wounds of my lovers.
One lover stands before me and her eyes look as deep as another lover's
and she says through hazel: "I am afraid of you." When my
body accidently arches in a swan pose, she looks at me and says:
"I can see why your other lovers would kill to keep you." My
brown-eyed lover is inscrutable above me. She plays me like a keyboard,
says: "You are too good to be true," her palpitations audible.
I am too good to be true though I give her myself for complex reasons,
none of which inspires awe. All my lovers got sober in 1980, 1985, 1990,
renewing themselves like phosphorus in the bone, linings of the intestine.
My lovers are so fragile! They love to fish and throw the fish back in,
to wash their hair in the trout stream—and look, every one of them
sits beside me as I write and says: "I love it when you write about me."
My lovers are systematic about control. One hoots out the window at women
beneath the El train. One hints at a liaison with Calvin, an old buddy

who wears panty hose. One is chasing her ex-girlfriend
up the stairs at an AA dance. We are all fighting now, my lovers and I,
fighting on Broadway in New York, Broadway in Chicago,
wherever there is a Broadway my lovers and I will be fighting.
Listen to our voices as they rise above the Hudson, above Lake Michigan.
I went to California without a lover. I rented a white Cavalier, this part is true,
and drove into high desert, far above sea and prairie. It was heady,
all that driving and calculation. I was counting my lovers. I was thinking
I might fall off a cliff on Highway 1, plunge into turquoise.
My mind danced like pollen in stilled water. I thought:
At this very moment my organs are replacing themselves—I am no more
fixed in time and space than Minnie Mouse! Even my priceless DNA
exists for a few short months, exchanging itself with earth and star.
Why, my old heart is probably fodder for lungfish and sponge,
my lovers planted at sea like treasure, their tiny eyes blinking light.

Lavabo manus meas

They say it's the iron in the blood that resists transformation.

It is also said that no creature can learn that which his heart has no shape to hold.

When she left him alone he found women who douched,
women with eel-skin legs and simpler schedules,
women obsessed with pumice and Q-Tips.

It is said that she lay in bed three days and two nights while her body slept off enough pills to kill a horse and he entered her regularly, and on the third day she awoke to the sound of water breaking and left her bed to begin a new life.

The best casserole in the world has no avocado. Therefore the following is written:

1. Chop some leftover meat.
2. Cook some noodles.
3. Sauté some onion and green pepper.
4. Mix it all together with a can of Campbell's Cream of Something Soup and a small amount of horseradish.

Bake at 350 degrees for one hour.
(Do not forget the horseradish or the casserole will be ordinary.)

There were nights of apple pies made with macs from upstate and enough cinnamon to make you cry. Days of attic living on Maple down the street from the folks with the Disney characters on their front lawn and the artificial deer. Near the river where you could see the nuclear power plant and get the willies thinking about it. And Bear Mountain where they went on their first date and she couldn't wait to have sex with a man who made love as if his life depended on pleasing her and it did.

It is written that only a pig can see the wind and that the wind is red.

Cannibal women in the avocado jungle of death step from behind the waterfall and their breasts are enormous. You could hide in those breasts for days, thinking only of guacamole. (Add chopped tomatoes, cloves of garlic crushed beneath a pestle made of stone, juice of a lemon, and you have the kind of guacamole men die for.)

He thought: casseroles, chipped beef, shrimp if you can get it.

She thought: *guacamole*—and disappeared like garlic into avocado, piquant as death, quiet as the whoosh of creation.

Called "Crass" by a Suitor during a Radically Conservative Moment in History, Helen Counsels Her Body

For Kathy Lewis

It's never been as terrifying as this, my
swan throat, my channeled song,

don't close around indelicacy, those
ill-bred words the size of ova and sperm,

or gag before your children, saying
sorry, you'd quite forgotten your chaste

beseeming self. You were launched
in blood and shit, my dainty nose,

yeast and phlegm, your Mom,
of steaming, burping, stinking Earth,

cursed God and all the little gods,
her gift your slimy farting flesh. My

quiet tongue, foaming ice, say something
coarse to part the seas, something viscous

and rank with generosity. We're
dissolving in the backwash, my fine

becoming lips, you can find men
hanging in the eaves like censored truths,

further and further from their souls.
Ears, delicate as a piano's upper reach,

listen for the suck of dirt and the polished
places left to uncivilize. Allow

the base, the shattered, the raw obscene
to enter your bones and save them.

Slow Dance

You were egalitarian with the sleaze you perpetrated, loving
transsexual and coed alike, so shy in your approach, no one
suspected your blue eyes. And when you sat barechested,
losing weight before me on the floor of One Eighty-Eight, I
never doubted you were crazy, not perverted after all, as
you continued to snap shots of showgirls in angular poses
and hunt all over Ossining for a large man of color to co-create
with your best friend's wife. Did I miss something our first date
on Bear Mountain? You knew so much about rattlesnakes and bats,
your darkness matched my light like sides of a clown suit.
I only gave you to the doctors and the cops because I feared
myself and the damage I seemed to be doing you, sucking
fat from your bones, hair right off your head—no one
deserves such power, wonder child, no matter what you say.
And yes I once slept with someone else while you were dying.
Remember the night you called me bitch slut whore and said
we'd both be better off dead? Not that night. The next.

Self-Portrait with Disasters

Imagine. I once walked the entire length
of Croton-on-Hudson in Hurricane Bob because
I liked the smell of ozone and destruction.
Then fell into snow so deep I drowned,
but that was in a dream, and since then,
the only thing I fear is waking. Now
when people hate me they say I must think
I'm powerful. The man who shot himself
in Missoula, on the other hand, had no power.
Once, he said, he saw his wedding mattress
floating down Broadway in South Yonkers.
His wife had thrown it out and a flood rose
and loosened it from the trash. I thought,
how amazing that Broadway stretches
from Albany to Battery Park and back again,
that beneath my feet lies the bedrock
of a shifting continent, above my head,
dust of a trillion dying stars. In fact,
I myself am suspended in the devastation.
For this moment only, I am the light.

During the Eclipse I Remember You Sent Me *Playboy*

R. Quentin, have you died of that cynical scissor you harbored
in your intestine so young, pallbearer of holy ghosts, beer-fed martyr

of Bronx and '68, oh chug-a-lug oh centerfold? Have you died your
premed *nihil* death, sacred organs rotting in your schoolboy crush

haughty as a pyramid with crushable butts and roaches,
naked elbows the base of your sluicing smile sipping Rheingold

through sordid smoke, brown teeth coy as baby boys in pink blankets?
Have you died of something grand but short—impulse on the IRT,

line on a mirror, gang activity where you played shield for someone
younger than you were when all I had to do was stop blushing

and I'd have smacked you with my virgin palm? Insomnia? Mating?
Has a small shard of glass entered your pinkie on a Saturday AM,

traveled quietly to your heart your heart your heart and on the fourth
hole by the pond in front of mallards you went down clutching

cash thinking: *My life as it flashes before me is nothing.* I've dreamt
of addressing you from *Playboy.* R., I would say, Look how my breasts

outmaneuver you, my vagina opens and closes on your sorry tongue,
religion's redundant, and see how I am sugar for you here

and here—page 81 ultimate diva. I know you were afraid to wish,
but if you dared would it be to sink yourself beyond the slick

of your subscriptions? It's true there is an eclipse occurring
as you occurred for one lunar moment of my coed career, worlds

fading with sadness, insanity in the alley, slivers of exquisite dark.
You told me: *You are blind from the sun, you are already fucking blind.*

Swan Lake

I

The Canada geese preen
along the lake's west end,
notice our passing
like old women on a porch.
A few murmur. One growls lightly.
Monarchs flit around our legs,
refusing to land.

Something in my hand
betrays me. I speak in tongues:
You fly to the highest branch,
balance like a hawk.
The lake reflects your eyes.
I want you.
Everything I say sounds like that.

I I

We lie beneath a beech
that weeps light and rain.
Our lips sing nonsense.
Our fingers play like children.

You draw two faces in the earth,
one with stars on the cheek,
one with tears, tell me:
Choose both.

III
The night swells around us.
Our voices, tense with lightning,
create a new silence.
Tree frogs surrender their bows,
crickets hush. Your shadow

emerges among the fireflies,
soft-edged, reflecting the moon.
I start, as if seeing you
for the first time, ask myself:
Who's the arrow and who's the swan?

The Sculpture Garden

Deirdre was almost ebony. She washed your boxers
and folded them neatly inside your backpack.
When I came home from the Cape, you'd painted our bedroom
black. A black box, you said. You lay down in the black box
and cried until your legs spun out around you, kicking me
hard like a dancer's. *Melissa*'s skin was chocolate mousse—

gorgeous, you said, and your voice hunkered down
as if she were your fur coat. She took you
to a dungeon on Thanksgiving. You both ate turkey
then she invited you to remove her blouse and hurt her.
The last time you saw her she said, "You're bald!"
And you flushed beneath your glossy scalp.

Maya the Carpenter was a buddy of yours.
You told me she came to you naked once
but you turned her down. I imagine her white matte shoulders
on an island in the Atlantic, how she taught you stars
are real and nothing is more sacred than wood. She said
you needed someone like me, and I felt proud.

The Ivory Soap Girl was a quick study.
I heard her call your name from Dojo's and watched you
fly inside the How Club, smirking. As she walked away
she looked back and shrugged, red hair singeing in the sun.
She was an actress, off-Broadway, semifamous.
You said you'd done nothing but sketch her. And *Eva*

posed between *The Woman in Kente Cloth with Extensions*
and *Kat*, who was your first Chicago sculpture,
an accountant by day who gave us her phone number
as a gesture of welcome. *Eva* had enormous freckled breasts
and liked to rub them against you. You held your cupped
hands out in front of you to demonstrate their size.

It's true—I'd always loved the delicacy of your hands,
the way they held me as if I were priceless.

Toy Car

Slippery as the word *deserve*. How the Catholic never gets washed out of you, the temple crushed completely. Once my husband brought home a little car. It fit beside the sleds and carriages like a toy for someone bigger than a toddler, smaller than a rock star. My husband deserved it, he said, and who was I to doubt him knowing as I did how his mother lifted him into her lap and pressed against his small back, the names of her troubles seared in his skin like Latin in the mind of a ten-year-old. *Introibo ad altare Dei.* I will go in to the altar of God. *Ad Deum qui laetificat juventutem meam.* To God who is the joy of my youth. I couldn't help the way I felt about toy cars and Bangladesh. The Jesuit in my book bag wrote on the board a thousand times: It's harder for a rich man, etc. . . . . The Sister of Sorrow in my lunch box crossed herself and thrust her hands up her cavernous sleeves. I had great ideas, my essays on the poor rivaled Merton and Marx. I was tortured by the hair shirt of my nondesires, I was living on the mountain and I couldn't get down. I lay beside my husband at night and thought: Who is this man who deserves such a tiny automobile that costs more to fix than food for a family of six in the South Bronx for a whole year? I thought: I am too tired to deserve anything and look, how shameless my rich husband, how wild his hair blows on the winds of Westchester in his toy car with the luscious leather seats big enough for him and someone else.

The West Room

There was once a Christmas when there was no Christmas tree
and the mom had a boyfriend and a rose between her teeth
and she left the children to decorate the spindly ficus and they did.
Tiny foil balls and felt ribbon. There was a twelve-inch
black-and-white TV playing the yule log and Nat King Cole.
And the landlord was spying on the mom as she went out the door,
and on the children stealing cookie decorations from his wife's collection—
nonpareils, green sugars, delicate snowflakes from West Germany.
He'd been waiting for the mom to really screw up. He'd been waiting
like a peeping tom in the azaleas, like Wile E. Coyote on a precipice
of sandstone, like an engorged teenager in Central Park.

There was once an Easter when the smallest girl's head was a playground
for lice. The mom took her last five dollars and bought the special shampoo
called Quell and she washed the little head under the tub faucet.
Then they all bent over, one by one, the mom, the boyfriend, the older girl
who loved nonpareils, they bent white and naked as gravestones,
their spines curved like thumbnails, and when the last louse was purged
from the heads of Ossining and every pearly nit dead on its shaft of hair,
the mom and the boyfriend made love in the north room. Where
they loved the hydrangea peeling off the attic walls and they loved
their spicy-smelling scalps and they made love quietly so the landlord
would not hear them and be jealous and tell the mom to leave.

The landlord screamed at her. *Where is your toilet brush? I knew*
you were a pig and a whore. How can you clean a toilet without a brush?
The boyfriend was gone, the children packing in the south room.
The mom was trying not to cry as she showed the landlord her Playtex gloves
and began to explain how she got down on her knees like this

and dipped her gloved hand into the icy water, how she was careful
to throw the gloves away when they got even a pin-sized hole,
how nothing escaped her practiced eye—not the drop of man-urine
on the underside of the seat, not the brown blood up under the rim,
not the dust on the base—and see, she used Lysol which they promise
kills every germ on contact and Comet Cleanser, look, with bleach.

There was a Thanksgiving when the cord that led from the plug
to the space heater scorched a line like a black snake into the cheap carpet,
when the children were sitting down to fresh cranberry relish
at their father's new house, and the mom was looking around her
frightened by the silence and the odor of the almost-horrible fire.
In the attic was a room without floorboards and Sheetrock
with broken windows that let in breezes and smelled dusty and safer
than the rest of the house. She tried to think which of the landlord's rooms
was beneath this one. The boys' bedroom, the sewing room. Jesus,
you can see the Hudson, she thought, sitting there
until every small light between her and the river came on.

A Story of Stonewall

June 27, 1968, NYC

A story of Stonewall goes like this: On the night of Judy Garland's funeral I was being raped by a man I'd met at Christmas in red velvet. It was something he would never remember, the kind of incident Judy would have endured in a haze of booze, ossified from the waist down, goofy the moment before, as if the bankruptcy rumors were all true. The amazing thing was his penis—tiny and senseless, it went in and out like a needle and what was I doing this whole time? *This is the end of my dreams,* I would have thought dramatically, and it was. After the hive of gays exploded on the city and, even though Judy was laid in state, I continued straight for nineteen years. Some men think she was special, misunderstood the way *they* were, all that dandruff you can say about a star who dies thin and fingered as a Kleenex. To me she will always be the leader of wind and slipper, the child who scraped jelly from a jar with a dull knife, a proud mustache of milk.

The Man Who Killed Himself to Avoid August

That night you looked like a little androgyne in your silk tie
and braids that touched your breasts or biceps depending
on the way the wind blew in Washington Square Park.
I was femmed-out in my new skirt with the built-in wrinkles
and queasy from just missing that glass of Dewars,
remember? *Why'd you want to go and do that for, you crazy?*
This is how crazy we were: I'd almost drowned in an ounce of scotch
and you'd almost slugged me. August: Too hot for some folks.
I had a friend who killed himself to get around it. You'd
been reminiscing about the addicts you were once fond of,
how you lost your virginity on the front seat of a Plymouth
to a disease-free white boy from Brooklyn
where your grandmother kept clean towels and enough change
to get you sober and back to Manhattan.
Behind you were two whispering waitresses,
the type I never trusted with Jersey accents and enough mental slack
to balance out Kerouac, their interest piqued
by the way you leaned over and kissed my hand. Oh,
honey, any clue how long it takes Irish blood to reach fever pitch?
When I was six, I tripped a toddler who looked
just like the Betsy-Wetsies yukking it up near the steam machine.
I was sitting angelically beside our picture window
while Poe chased the milk truck down the road
and my mother brewed coffee for her guests and my foot
shot out. Just like that, the kid down and wailing. That night
the air was a drunk's thick tongue, people circling
slow as sharks on MacDougal. The man who killed himself
sounded like a movie star from Yonkers and played with gender.

He was searching for his Dean Moriarty, he would say,
and once walked due west and slid quietly into the river.
That night the waitresses were cutting up Manhattan
into huge pieces of pie. You could feel the blade,
you could take the air in your hand and squeeze Kahlua
into your iced cappuccino. Subcultures swarmed. Some
blended in like cream, some debated drug cost near the teeter-totter.
We were swimming underwater, slick and seasoned as rats.
We were gaining on the waitresses from Jersey where
the Palisades grew all the way down to the center of the earth.

Femme-Butch Dialogue

There is the Christian martyr with the one arrow, the martyr
with many arrows, we ourselves have been arduously trained

for death by arrows or fire. We're sitting in the lard-free café
near Emmanuel Lutheran on Broadway in New Town

where martyrdom is passé, at least we no longer remember
why we should prepare ourselves for boiling oil

when All the Lovers I Have Loved and All the Lovers
You Have Loved walk by in one new-physics moment—

release of time and space—the lovers unsuspecting,
heading for The Closet across the street for Diet Coke.

We eat enchiladas verdes, we eat the whole thing, talking
of butch and femme and what that means and you say:

Why would you want a woman when you can have a man?
I recall wanting love so badly I don't even think I cared

it was a man back in my young days when men were still boys.
You say you were tomboyish from the start

so when you see a woman like me who is such
a woman, a real woman, you say—whatever that is, I say—

you give away your soul and that's why butches
are afraid of femmes deep down and never feel quite equal.

I remember in fifth grade, St. Theresa's School,
how the boys betrayed each other when the girls walked by,

our power radiating like golden fruit, energy out there
shining for the bees and all the groping sticky fingers

wanting us and all we had to give, our store of honey.
The first time I ever roared at my ex-husband

I stood at the sink and said I hate you over and over
until his face turned red and all the years settled upon him

like a mountain. The woman who saved me from him
was lovely and dark. I loved the way she wanted me wildly, we

were women in the world together, and isn't that
too good to be true? I said to him because he held me—

You can't keep me under this house with my shoes sticking out,
my legs with their circulation cut off at the ankles.

Failing martyrdom at forty was nevertheless just in time.
Carol and I eating enchiladas in New Town where

All the Lovers We Have Ever Loved come and go as they please,
arrows cutting paths of light around their flesh.

A Chorus of Horizontals

You're scanning New York radio in your old Honda on the Saw Mill
Parkway headed south around Hastings where the snow-swollen river

angles up near traffic and my god you've got four webbed feet gliding
right in front of your face practically landing on your windshield,

and you flinch and shut your eyes, your heart's percussive, and they've
got the nerve to say *honk*. Then you're fishing near Muscoot Farm

with a young angler who's dead now, this time you're shirt-free in the dusk
and he's scared someone might see your small breasts, when that *V*

arrives from places south low enough for you to hear the commander
set the pace, the brigade of beaks holler back, and you're tickled by

the alarmed trumpet of a straggler: *Wait for me, oh fellas, oh kin.*
And you hug the man to keep him grounded. Those trips with your kids to

Tarrytown Lake. Who knew the birds would be so rude they'd chomp your
fingers too? Wherever you go they follow, slick Harpies, as if you're

their star, their hunger. They all point to you. You believe this
and it keeps you alive through winter after winter when, missing them,

you go down to the steely Chicago at the end of your ice-encrusted
impossible street and throw bread upon the water.

Furious Cooking

For Susan and Vanessa

It's the kind of cooking where before you begin
you dump the old beef stew down the toilet

and flush it thinking, good, watching
gravy splatter on the shiny white tiles.

Where the chicken spread-eagled on the butcher block
could be anyone and you don't even bother to say

thanks for your life, chicken, or regret the way
the little legs remind you of just that.

Where the bay leaves aren't eased in but thrown
voilà into sizzling olive oil which

burns the *poulet* nicely along with the onions
alerting the fire alarm and still you think,

good, let the landlord worry I'll burn this bitch down.
It's the kind of cooking that gives your family

agita, big Italian-style pain, even if it's only
fricasee the way your Nana used to make it.

She was so pissed she painted her kitchen ceiling red!
Remember the Irish soda-bread chicken and all those

green veggies in heavy cream your poor mother
yelled so loud about, oh, the calories! Furious

cooking, the kind where hacking the *pollo*
to bits with no names, you look up to see the windows

steamed like a hothouse. In fact, it's so hot
you strip to bare skin and now you're cooking mad

and naked in just that bartender's smock with the screw
you'd like to stick into some big cork right now.

Cooking everyone can smell from the street. What
the fuck, they say, and hurry home to safe food, yours

a rank hint of ablution and sacrifice, although
no one recognizes the danger. I used to wonder

about the Portuguese woman on the first floor,
what that odor was that drifted up on Saturdays

into my own savory kitchen. How it permeated
Sunday and Monday as well, all that lethal food left

to boil on her big stove from the old country.
Now I know she was just furious cooking, that aroma was

no recipe you'd find in any country, a cross between
organs and feathers and spinal fluid and two eyes,

not to mention the last song in that chicken's throat
before it kicked the bucket in the snow in the prime

of life when all it ever wanted you could etch on a dime
and spin blithely into a crack in the kitchen table.

Notes

After Sinéad O'Connor Appears on *Saturday Night Live*, the Pope

On October 3, 1992, Irish singer-songwriter Sinéad O'Connor tore an 8-by-12-inch photograph of Pope John Paul II to pieces before a live audience. She had just finished her a capella song about racial, class, and child abuse and said, "Fight the real enemy." She was subsequently booed as well as cheered at a Madison Square Garden tribute to Bob Dylan on October 16.

Too Much Light Makes the Baby Go Blind, celebrating its seven-year run in 1995, is the Chicago theater phenomenon of the Neo-Futurists created by Greg Allen.

The quotes are from Barbara G. Walker's *The Women's Encyclopedia of Myths and Secrets* (Harper & Row, 1983).

Malleus Maleficarum

Malleus Maleficarum, or *The Witch's Hammer*, was a comprehensive witch hunter's handbook mandated by Pope Innocent VIII and written by Dominican inquisitors Heinrich Kramer and James Spreger. It was first published in Germany in 1486 and quickly spread throughout Europe, second only to the bible in sales until the publication of John Bunyan's *Pilgrim's Progress* in 1678. It was divided into three sections: the devil and his witches, how witches cast spells, and legal procedures for trying witches.

Information on *The Witch's Hammer*, the torture and burnings, etc., appears in Rosemary Ellen Guiley's *Witches and Witchcraft* (Facts on File, 1989) and Barbara G. Walker's *The Women's Encyclopedia of Myths and Secrets* (Harper & Row, 1983). Quotes in "Malleus Maleficarum 4" are taken from the latter.

Exquisite Corpse

Cadavre Exquis, a surrealist parlor game played by André Breton et al. in the '20s and '30s, takes its name from "the exquisite corpse shall drink the new wine," one of the more intriguing of the collaborative lines recorded.

Theories of Illusion

Written after inhaling Stephen Jay Gould's *The Panda's Thumb* (Norton, 1980).

A Single Subatomic Event

Jean Anouilh said, "I like reality, it tastes of bread."
All other italicized quotes are taken from Larry Dossey's *Space, Time, and Medicine* (Shambhala, 1982).

Cannibal Women in the Avocado Jungle of Death

The title is a 1988 comedy directed by J. D. Athens.
The idea for the first line comes from Dossey's *Space, Time, and Medicine.*
"No creature can learn that which his heart has no shape to hold" is a quote from *All the Pretty Horses* by Cormac McCarthy (Knopf, 1992).
The recipe is a variation on a Janet Bowe special, circa 1970.
Kerry Bacia found the idea about the pig in a Zora Neal Hurston story in *Of Mules and Men* (Harper & Row, 1990) and I, for one, believe it.

THE IOWA POETRY PRIZE WINNERS

1987
Elton Glaser, *Tropical Depressions*
Michael Pettit, *Cardinal Points*

1988
Bill Knott, *Outremer*
Mary Ruefle, *The Adamant*

1989
Conrad Hilberry, *Sorting the Smoke*
Terese Svoboda, *Laughing Africa*

1993
Tom Andrews, *The Hemophiliac's Motorcycle*
Michael Heffernan, *Love's Answer*
John Wood, *In Primary Light*

1994
James McKean, *Tree of Heaven*
Bin Ramke, *Massacre of the Innocents*
Ed Roberson, *Voices Cast Out to Talk Us In*

1995
Ralph Burns, *Swamp Candles*
Maureen Seaton, *Furious Cooking*

THE EDWIN FORD PIPER POETRY AWARD WINNERS

1990
Philip Dacey, *Night Shift at the Crucifix Factory*
Lynda Hull, *Star Ledger*

1991
Greg Pape, *Sunflower Facing the Sun*
Walter Pavlich, *Running near the End of the World*

1992
Lola Haskins, *Hunger*
Katherine Soniat, *A Shared Life*